THE FINAL
VOICEMAILS

MAX RITVO

THE FINAL VOICEMAILS

EDITED BY LOUISE GLÜCK

MILKWEED EDITIONS

Published 2018 by Milkweed Editions
Printed in Canada
Cover design by Mary Austin Speaker
Author photo by Ashley Woo
18 19 20 21 22 5 4 3 2 1
First Edition

Milkweed Editions, an independent nonprofit publisher, gratefully acknowledges sustaining support from the Jerome Foundation; the Lindquist & Vennum Foundation; the McKnight Foundation; the National Endowment for the Arts; the Target Foundation; and other generous contributions from foundations, corporations, and individuals. Also, this activity is made possible by the voters of Minnesota through a Minnesota State Arts Board Operating Support grant, thanks to a legislative appropriation from the arts and cultural heritage fund, and a grant from Wells Fargo. For a full listing of Milkweed Editions supporters, please visit milkweed.org.

Library of Congress Cataloging-in-Publication Data

Names: Ritvo, Max, 1990-2016, author. | Gluck, Louise, 1943- editor.
Title: The final voicemails / Max Ritvo ; edited by Louise Gluck.
Description: Minneapolis : Milkweed Editions, 2018.
Identifiers: LCCN 2017058089 (print) | LCCN 2018000244 (ebook) | ISBN
    9781571319906 (ebook) | ISBN 9781571315113 (cloth : acid-free paper)
Classification: LCC PS3618.I8 (ebook) | LCC PS3618.I8 A6 2018 (print) | DDC
    811/.6--dc23
LC record available at https://lccn.loc.gov/2017058089

Milkweed Editions is committed to ecological stewardship. We strive to align our book production practices with this principle, and to reduce the impact of our operations in the environment. We are a member of the Green Press Initiative, a nonprofit coalition of publishers, manufacturers, and authors working to protect the world's endangered forests and conserve natural resources. *The Final Voicemails* was printed on acid-free 100% post-consumer-waste paper by Friesens Corporation.

CONTENTS

II. Mammals

Editor's Note

Max Ritvo was a prodigiously gifted poet; toward the end of his life, he was also volcanically productive. Nothing he wrote was without flashes of brilliance, but many of these late poems would surely have been revised or jettisoned; it was slow work to sift out the very best. This he asked me to do—it seemed to me an essential labor lest the weaker poems dilute the stronger. What follows, obviously, reflects my judgment. Nothing has been revised; Elizabeth Metzger, Max's designated literary executor, suggested one minute cut.

I have chosen to include with these late poems a slightly abbreviated version of *Mammals*, Max's extraordinary undergraduate thesis. Some of these poems were imported to enlarge *Aeons* and *Four Reincarnations*; they are included here in their original forms, partly because they shape *Mammals* and partly because the small adjustments seem to me interesting. These poems also serve as a general reminder to readers, and to poets, that the work of twenty-year-olds is not necessarily practice work.

Cancer was Max's tragedy; it was also, as he was canny enough to see, his opportunity. Poets who die at twenty-five do not commonly leave bodies of work so urgent, so daring, so supple, so desperately alive.

This book has no dedication. Had he lived, I feel certain Max would have wished to honor his wife, Victoria, who gave his last years rare intensity and joy. He would have wished to thank his closest peer, Elizabeth Metzger. And always and ultimately his remarkable mother, Riva Ariella Ritvo, whose resourcefulness and passion bought him more time than he might otherwise have had. His teachers he thanked repeatedly in his magical work.

LOUISE GLÜCK

Clear, the doctor says to your heart
before bolting it.

She's saying this to clear away
everything else in the room.

Clear! I say, *Your heart is clear! Clear as a fishbowl!*

I.

THE FINAL VOICEMAILS (2016)

THE FINAL VOICEMAILS

1

I was told my proximity
to the toxin would promote
changes to my thinking, speech, and behavior.

My first thought was, of course,
for the child, the little girl,

but graceful, silent figures
in white suits flitted to her

and led her away by the shoulders, like two friends
taking a turtle from a pond.

My second thought was about pain,
the last thing visible
without our manners—

Or could there be an invisible peace
once the peace of the senses departs?

2

I'm glad she's gone, and not just for her sake:
without her I feel somehow better equipped
to be what I am becoming—

which is, I suppose, preoccupied.

Nobody ever tells you how *busy* loneliness is—

Every night I cover the windows in soap,
and through the night I dart
soap over any lick of light
that makes its way to my desk
or bed or the floor.

At first it was fear—an understanding that the light
was death, was the toxin,
though really the toxin was invisible,
they said, and came from the water.

But work blesses fear
like a holy man blessing a burlapped sinner,
saying *It is for you* and *Because of you,*

and in time the working mind
knows only itself, which is loneliness.

3

Dim sight now,
and each twitch flows
into a deep, old choreography.

Maybe a week ago, my arm banged the faucet,
and I danced
in the middle of the bathroom—
the entire final dance
from the tango class we took
at the gym in New Haven,
with the air as you.

I wasn't picturing you,
I didn't smell your damp hair—
don't imagine that I'm living
in memory.

Whatever I am, it is good at cutting meat.
The trick is: *That's blood.*
If you focus your fingers on feeling it,
you cannot mistake yourself for the animal,
who cannot feel; you never cut yourself
if you give your life to the blood you shed.

4

I know you've been waiting for disintegration,
but it just doesn't seem to be coming.

I need to go out to gather some berries.
No more meat: I've adopted your diet.

All this time, I thought my shedding
would expose a core,
I thought I would at least know myself,

but these mild passions, all surface, keep erupting now
like acne—or like those berries on a bush.

Don't ask me to name them—
I've never been that kind of guy.
Red berries—sour, sticky.
If you really want to know,
come here, just try them.

Red as earth,
red as a dying berry,
red as your lips,
red as the last thing I saw
and whatever next thing I will see.

THE SOUNDSCAPE OF LIFE IS CHARRED BY TINY BONFIRES

Two bedtimes ago, through my window,
I heard a cat get eaten.

As the cat split, it sounded like
a balloon string put to scissors

to make curls so the birthday boy
would smile extra wide.

Last night, by the same window,
I heard mostly my breath, inside of which

was a small baby suckling
my air for his milk.

When I bolted upright, the baby
grew up into a carpenter,

nailing his brains into the side of my lung
to babyproof the light switch.

Flip the switch and it lights
a picture of my emaciated, sore-ridden bum

for my breath to laugh at.
Why is my breath so unlike yours?

My ears? Why do I only hear such unnatural things?
Although, come to think of it, death is completely natural.

I'm just exasperated. Everywhere *life-sounds*
swarm this, our shared pond, like mating turtles.

Cars whoosh, schmoozers hum,
snakes spit poison, Martin and Martina say *yes*

and sob and hold, but my ears fill up instead
with eggshells cracked by the bumbling parents.

I cleaned my left ear out,
but my nail cut the drum.

It filled with water
and is deaf for now.

I'm leaving the right one dirty. No sudden changes.
Keep everything dry. Let it figure out a way to heal itself.

And me: just practice living with yourself deaf.
Sometimes your brain is as unwelcome

as muscles or guns. It's obvious to others. Maybe even
everyone. Don't wish for anything. Don't get organized.

Don't buy a book. Don't go to bed early.
Seek out beige, in foodstuffs and landscapes.

Chew gum if you're overwhelmed.
You're in this alone. That means there's nobody to stop you.

You're almost at the finish line.
But first, you have to pick a finish line.

DELPHI

Everyone asks you what the god thinks—
I want to know what *you* think.

Behind the temple, a short lady
bends in terror over a shallow pond's edge.

I tell her if she wants opinions
she has to get to the other side
and undress—a bamboo hedge
will tastefully obscure her

—peach and coconut flashes
behind vegetable prison bars—

that the prison is the mind,
that the pond is what we call thought.

She's not so short her hair
would get muddy—
only the washable robes
and sandals.

I get into the pond and point out a path of rocks,
and my bald head too,
so she may step across.

I tell her to think of my bald head
as a squeaky, dense pill
of white medicine.

She says, *Have you been reading Philosophy?*

Indeed, I have been reading Philosophy,
and I hate that she didn't have to think to notice
and grab her hem to drown her,

and instead we're in the temple
and she's dancing with the suitcase
I brought all the way from distant, homey Thrace

and the clothes sweetly perfumed with me
are a soul in the leather's misery

and I dive in the clothes and they stink and rot,
but that's just the god's thought.

Your mouth is sealing mine in the mud,

opposite heads from two underbellies
of the pond,

a difficult marvel
flashing in *your* (not the god's)
eyes, because I lied to you—

I have been reading not philosophy but *medicine*,
and my baldness is *not* wisdom,

and the pond is not thought, but *my* thought,
which is always on death, like your mouth,

and the mud is marriage lace,

and your opinions are newborn
hares and toads and musical nuggets,
stirring in your organs as the mud hardens.

QUIET ROMANCE

I am too weak for sexual urges anymore
but I yearn to be naked
all the time.

I want to urinate without
having to pull off
underpants—

The world wants me to know
it's okay to slip into and out
of her. She likes it.

When I die, make sure
Dad doesn't screw a hat on me
to keep the brains in.

And let nobody put a shirt on me.
Let death put her cool head
on my stomach for a listen.

I want every hole naked:
the pupils, nostrils, the two
below my gut. I want to listen back:

I can hear already
a roaring in the distance,
half salt, half horse,

I like this, I'm scared, but
so's the sound. We'll both
be guests.

EARTHQUAKE COUNTRY BEFORE FINAL CHEMOTHERAPY

For the first time, tonight
as I put my wife to bed
I didn't have to shove her off me.

She turned away in her sleep.

I wondered what was wrong with my chest.

I felt it, and the collarbone
spiked up, and where she'd rest
her cheek were ribs.

Who wants to cuddle a skeleton?

My skeleton wandered from the house
and out onto the street.

He came, after much wandering, to the edge of a bay
where a long bridge headed out—
the kind that hangs itself with steel

and sways as if the wind could take
away its weight.

There were mountains in the distance—
triangles of cardboard—
or perhaps the mist was tricking his eyes.

The instant the mist made him doubtful,
it turned to rain.

The rain covered everything. The holes
in his face were so heavy
he wondered if the water was thickening—
if he was leaching into them.

He panicked. Perhaps he was gunked up
with that disgusting paste,
flesh, all over again.

If I were alive I'd have told him
I was nothing like what he was feeling—

that the rain felt more like
the shell of a crab
than the way I'd held him.

That it felt more like him.

But I wasn't alive—
I was the ghost in the bridge
willing the cars to join me,

telling them that death was not wind,
was not weight,

was not mist,
and certainly not the mountains—

that it was the breaking apart,

the replacement of who, when, how, and where
with what.

When my skeleton looked down
he was corrupted

in the femur by fracture,
something swelling within.

Out of him leaked pink moss.
Water took it away.

MY BATHTUB PAL

I am writing you from the bathtub
where I am trying to ease my joints.
The pain seems to move from the front half
of a joint to a back half.

I can't track it across my body.

My pain is mild but deep—like it's reminding
my body of something it once was.
It thinks I'm a baby:

Look at the oatmeal prepared for you daily,
and your electric blankets,
and it's me you choose to lavish your attention on?

You have so much more than me,
though you had me first, when you were a Worm.

This pain thinks thinking is idiotic, embarrassingly juvenile,
and I'm proof of that.

And it's not even the pain foremost,
it is the story of me in pain that is paining me.

I am possessed with self-pity,
and it is expressing itself
out of my mouth. It sounds like a whole flock of sheep suddenly

realizing the flock is an imposed externality.

AMUSE-BOUCHE

It is rare that I
have to stop eating anything
because I have run out of it.

We, in the West, eat until we want
to eat something else,
or want to stop eating altogether.

The chef of a great kitchen
uses only small plates.

He puts a small plate in front of me,
knowing I will hunger on for it
even as the next plate is being
placed in front of me.

But each plate obliterates the last
until I no longer mourn the destroyed plate,

but only mewl for the next,
my voice flat with comfort and faith.

And the chef is God,
whose faithful want only the destruction
of His prior miracles to make way
for new ones.

MY NEW FRIEND

1

It was two months ago, walking to the corner store
to feed my wife KitKats.

The man had almost no eyebrows
and his suit seemed to be of perfunctory navy.
But when I got closer I noticed
acorns and flowers stitched in the same color.

He said *I'm the Soul Eater*,
so I assumed he wasn't real.

My wife couldn't see him, but soon
large quantities of flour
went missing, and eggs too—
there were bite marks on the bags.

For her sake I set out rodent traps.
I killed all the blood and brains in the building,

but still, the food went, and then the springs
in our daughter's bed.

2

Last week I saw him in the bathtub:
he'd filled it with quarters and was popping them
into his mouth.

I thought you were here to eat my soul,
not my money, I tell him,
and he shoots back, *What's the difference in a case like this?*

I ask him if he is death. He says no.
I ask if he *knows* death—again I get a no.

He nods his head at his navel, obscured by quarters:
You're not exactly what I had in mind either . . .

3

It seems now that whatever I look upon with intense love
goes sour. My favorite purse was blasted
to powder and clasps, my blue fish blanket
blacked out with holes.

I argue with my daughter over her declining grades
so she eats in her room, where I can't slip up
and look at her. I kiss my wife's feet and hands
only, and with my eyes shut tight.

At night is worst, when I look at nothing.
I dream I am in his stomach,
walking through an unearthly pink cave.

Above me and around me, all the eaten souls are becoming flesh
like little fairy lights hardening into raisins.

So this is death—the irreducible is simply
the last thing to be reduced, I think to myself.

4

There are long stretches now where there is no language
in my mind. A pleasure is there

but I couldn't describe it except as the general current
one feels through all forms
of refreshment: the down of sleep, the up of water.

I've talked to the man quite a bit at this point—
and he assures me this isn't dying. He tells me

dying is only one of many exits a mind can take.
Some minds, the ones who die,

are like a family.
They leave the restaurant all together
and go to sleep in the same home. This is never up for discussion,
never even thought about—
it's what gets them through the meal.

But some minds are like single friends
set up on blind dates: *Call me when you get in safe!*
the friends say as the meal ends.

And if they *do* call, it's a wonder, the phone
sending an angel into the house. Silence
is more the norm. Either way, the world beyond
the house is remote and distorted.

No one knows when anyone else truly sleeps.
No one knows when they themselves sleep.

If no one is there to correct your imagination,
how is it not the world?

It's one way to avoid Hell! the man says,
and he starts to laugh again
but the laugh becomes a cough—
he looks thin these days.

5

When my heart stops, it will be the end of certain things,
but not the end of things itself.

Sure, my smile is useful, but a chair is useful too.
In the end, I love chairs, and I love dogs,
and I'll *be* chairs, and I'll *be* dogs,
and if I am ever a thought of my widow
I'll love being that.

Two weeks ago, I hosted a large dinner for my friend's birthday.
Her husband was out of town, as was my wife.
Something about it was ill-composed,
and it wasn't the restaurant's fault.
The food and service were impeccable—
it's like I sat people to maximize silence.

Some people were born to be guests. Like me.
Next time, I told her, you pick the spot.

UNCLE NEEDLE

Today my uncle gave me the death I always wanted.

He touched me with a couple needles
and my arms went to the bed

and my legs felt like they went deeper
into the ground two stories below.

I noticed half my life was floating
in cotton. Almost all of life is floating

if you count the air beneath floors
or the tar above earth.

For a moment, my nose
had to deal with so much violence

just there, in the air trying to reach me,
that there was no time to think my violent thoughts.

And my uncle sat in a chair by the bed
and thought tenderly of me—he didn't ask me to think,

to keep thinking. But there will be a next death.
You can't hold a cut shut.

You can't stitch a heart into beating.
Why can't everyone be more like uncle?

DINNER IN LOS ANGELES, RAINING IN JULY

The black night is a sea urchin.
The sea urchin is my mother
moving on spiny feet,
meat clotting with her desires.

But meat isn't the only thing
that moves the feet—
the cold sky puckers them,
shafts of gnats tickle them,
and the aroma of all things burns on the ground.

The feet won't obey her.
Every foot has a hunch in the wilderness.

*

As the sprinklers brutalize the window,
the sun setting into city light,

you ask to see my plate,
my plate, still studded with green beans.

Thinking fast, I pitch up my voice into a story
about Dad trying to plug up gophers in the yard.

About how when Prajapati opened his mouth,
he birthed the fire that eats fathers—
like a hose spraying gophers into his face.

*

The only stars left
are mothers.

Behind the urchin of the night is the ocean of the night.
Mother says, *Eat something: I'm giving up on you.*

*

Excusing myself for the bathroom,
I walk out the kitchen door and into the wet yard.

Above me are stars
but no constellations.

They won't join tonight—
even with their own kind.

I think, had they worn
the woolly clouds as wigs,
nobody would've mistaken
their bright eyes for bald spots—
not even themselves, poor critical things.

ANATOMIC AND HYDRAULIC CHASTITY

Instead, the world is olive oil,
and I'm a repulsive water sack.

Pleasure? My greatest pleasure?
Getting out of the way.

Sometimes I can almost feel
what the world would be like without me:
like an olive-green paperback
shutting a perfect story flat—
no longer crimped by
a spasmodic paper clip miming
the shape of his genitals
with his nauseated, skinny body.

O to be full of olive oil,
O for the skull to be a case
of olive oil,

for the kiss to mingle freely
the oils in two skulls,
for a telepathic love in the shared mouth:
a slow whorl spooling from the craniums
to the ceramic lips.

O for meals to be as peaceful
as groping out for rosemary—
the hands unearthly, frictionless,
in a garden.

Keep aggrieving me, oily flavors
in your curvaceous bowl,
your charwoman, a pillar of salt.

Don't leave Maxcat alone
or I'll have to see exactly
what I have in store for me.

YOUR NEXT DATE ALONE

The stage is empty.
How do you fill it?
With music.

The words will be the play,
and the tune will be the body
carrying the words,
shaking with tears,

the towel torn
so what he'd like hidden
is exposed—

where his flesh is like a bruised heart.

If you wish to see me
you'll have to sing.

I will soon have none
of the ways earth plays

along with the soul:
no grass, no wind.

NOBODY ASKED ANYTHING

Nobody asked anything, and then we suffered
and our words hooked up to the sky

and there were questions. Questions led to science,
which led to pills. But we suffered and

there is no pill to treat time.
Douse the fire and the candle sheds water.

Under new light, the dark, I write,
the hot fat drips lumping

and water dripping now
over the columns of fat it made.

Always movement, even the ground moves,
nobody asked anything but still

the bodies hook up: when we run out of air
we fill with foul gas.

DOWN WITH THE LANDLORD

Strange changes all over the house—
ants living off water alone
in the bathroom,
the walls going gold
with glue.

*

Tomorrow they will seal off a bedroom
in my body, a bedroom for wind,
a lobe of lung.

Wherever they dump it,
I will still feel its room
in my body.

*

The new tenant bolts up from the bed
and hurls himself at the sealed door,
a black folder clutched in one hand,
a saw clutched in the other—

*

Don't worry, body: I'm coming for you,
I will fuse you back up
into a happy home.

Let room mean death or room mean life,
but let the room always be full.
Down with the Landlord!
He is leaving you empty!

DECEMBER 29

I found myself unable to consume
the scallops after reflection—
their whole lives were
eating and suffocating.

This is much sadder than tortured people—
in extreme pain we leave our bodies
and look down to commit the pain
to memory like studious angels.

The waiter brought me two fortune cookies.
One future was traumatic enough.
I decided to open just one cookie—
the one on my right side.

It said in blue on a thin white strip,
You must learn to love yourself.

*

The cookie was much less sweet
than my psychiatrist.

Earlier that day he said he was proud
that as my tumors grow
my self-loathing seems to shrink.

My teeth made the cookie into blades
that cut my tongue, and I spat it out.

I was seized with a question for Dr. Possick,
but he was on the other coast, fast asleep.

I would have asked,
If all of me is the part that's loving
what is left to love?

*

I was suddenly overwhelmed with certainty
that the second cookie could answer my question.

I imagined the paper as a body—
a second body for me,

baking in a clay oven
half beneath it and half overhead.

I didn't open the cookie though.
I have to grow up at some point—

my imagination can't always be kicking fate
as if it were the floor at a stupid party.

*

But when you decide someone has something to say
their silences speak to you too—

The cookie's clear wrapper had a rooster printed on it.
The lamp's reflection made a little sun
clutched by the talons, deep in the clay:

What is left to love
is the part of you that is already dead.

*

The dead part of me
is very busy preparing heaven for the rest.

He envisions it as a dream cemetery:
no rabbis, wildflowers and scrub everywhere,
rolling hills with nothing marked,

computer chips clipped to the ears of the dead
so that loved ones can visit the exact spot.

He is unskilled with his hands,
but he's moneyed and shouts well.

It's hard to love people committed to projects:
when I tell him he's abusing the labor

he smiles proudly and says, *God can only do good,*
I can do good and bad.

TUESDAY

We haven't moved from this pier in a couple years.
All we need to do to be happy is point out fish.

Sure, we're just pointing at ripples,
but we know they're fish

because a long time ago we ate an oyster,
and every time a fish sees another,

you and me get fed again. Elizabeth,
when you put your hands to the scales

the senses lose weight and
a new full that doesn't hurt me

can last in my stomach. The bulk of the meat
you thin into a braid of arrows,

and the gills, the difficult scissors taken inside
to breathe, they're just wide arrows.

A kind that points—
like a hand tremoring

because there's a past being pointed to
that already understood the present.

NAME MY TIME OF DEATH AND SEE WHAT I DO TO YOU

Time's up. Break's over. So I put the doctors on the floor again
and ask them for a diagnosis.

I've been keeping the doctors in line
on a little tan balance beam—

Whenever they reach the end I pluck them
up by the collar.

There's a little sadist in me—or boys
will be boys. I think I just got tired

of bad news, and each time
less air getting into my lungs.

Over time, I've corrupted their gaits.
Now it's their floor time. I command the docs to circle me

and with prognostic spoons plug up the holes
where they used to show me my body.

But their legs can only slam forward, crimped
and insanely looped like mine.

Down they bash into the ground,
screaming like a baby realizing it's a monkey.

The diagnosis comes in underwhelming:
We can't tell if you're going to live

or if the background image
looks an awful lot like you.

My milk is running brown, but what they're calling
cells in it are more like feathers up close.

I think there's something in me
more horrible than they're detecting—

I think I'd kill to stay alive,
at least myself,

and if you can't accept that
you don't know the angel in my blood.

What if I ran out of a body to give you?
What would you let me take from you?

A star, a raft, a bloody cloth, a bloody cloud,
my body, my body, I'm running for you only,
and my fear is the most beautiful thing I have ever seen.

CACHEXIA

Today I woke up in my body
and wasn't that body anymore.

It's more like my dog—
for the most part obedient,
warming to me
when I slip it Goldfish or toast,

but it sheds.
Can't get past a simple sit,
stay, turn over. House-trained, but not entirely.

This doesn't mean it's time to say goodbye.

I've realized the estrangement
is temporary, and for my own good:

My body's work to break the world
into bricks and sticks
has turned inward.

As all the doors in the world
grow heavy
a big white bed is being put up in my heart.

BOY GOES TO WAR

His father told him never start writing
or reading in the middle of a book.

There's a title, don't go on without one.
And he didn't go on without one—he had the title Private.

This was life's taproot—the obedient
boy began always at the beginning.

Books start out with what the boy calls Beauty:
The boat's still in port. The cat's alive. Pantry's packed.

Even present tense has some of the grace of past tense,
what with all the present tense left to go.

Usually, by the first page or second,
a relationship emerges between text and title.

Some of the words blur on the page
and the key ones glow,

as does the title, and a fat red arrow
with two heads connects them. Yum.

It was like owning something. The way
when he paid for a fine hat and put it on,

he felt a circuit through the rim and top
and sides, swilling gray hat blood.

And he felt like his heart controlled this circuit
remotely, via microchip.

If a book could not service him with this truth,
which was all the pleasure in the world,

he would usually stop reading.
He saw the end of very few books anyway—

Who needs two climaxes? After that intense sensation
the book always changed. It was like looking

at a plate of food he'd half-eaten
that had rendered him bloated and nauseous.

Now he is on marches. Now his gun
makes a nest in his arm crook

with nasty red welts for straw.
Now his rear leaks smelly water all day.

His whole life he has balanced himself
on an absurdly slender proscenium

and as he continues to edge out
he can't tell if it isn't maybe a gangplank.

He doesn't like the switch-up.
What's out there? he wonders,

in what he'll call *ocean* for now.
To his right is an alligator.

But the head-ridge has no bone.
It's propped up instead by fumes:

rich, dark, and pungent. Far off,
men are cradling cracked dolphins.

Arrows of fire shoot out the blowholes.
The wounds bleed silver.

Perhaps they are connecting to a title in the sky.
But he's not seeing any of these things.

The world is mostly brown and black
and smells like a rotting fridge.

What is it? What is it? Is it a hand?
Is it an eye? Is it a hat?

CENTAUR MUSIC

All their words
have been spoken before
by human mouths.

They have to put music to the words
to make them mean anything
other than what someone has already felt.

If you said I've got the world on a string,
they would dance against our fences,
grating themselves bald as cheese.

Their lives are full of admissions
you'd rather not make.

Each Centaur's music is different according
to where they are joined.

You are the only one for me,
sings my Centaur,
horse up to the lips,
singing almost all-horse music.

Even her lady nose is shaped
like a horse cantering,
or an alien ship whining exhaust,

and I am a single gold ring,
snug round the azure planet of her words—
which, in her spaceship, she is fleeing from.

LEISURE-LOVING MAN SUFFERS UNTIMELY DEATH

You ask why the dinner table has been so quiet.
I've felt, for a month, like the table:

holding strange things in my head
when there are voices present.

And when the voices die,
a cool cloth and some sparkling spray.

I'm on painkillers around the clock,
and I fear it's always been

just the pain talking to you.

The last vision was of the pain leaving—
it looked just like me as it came out

of my mouth, but it was holding a spatula.
It was me if I had learned to cook.

The pain drifted to the kitchen.
He hitched himself to the oven, was a centaur

completed by bread, great black loaves
bursting from the oven,

and then the vision vanished.
I followed, and stood where he had stood.

The knives rustled in the block,
the pans clacked overhead.

I'm sterile from chemo,
and thought of that.

Sure, I wish my imagination well,
wherever it is. But now

I have sleep to fill. Every night
I dream I have a bucket

and move clear water from a hole
to a clear ocean. A robot's voice barks,

This is sleep. This is sleep.
I'd drink the water, but I'm worried the next

night I'd regret it.
I might need every last drop. Nobody will tell me.

II.

MAMMALS (2013)

LAJUWA FORGETS HOW TO LOVE

The story of the Yoruban chamberlain who donned the veil
of the dead king to become king

I'm told I'm bad at love poems
so, as a backup, I became King.

I was the chamberlain in Aworokolokin's court.

It was thankless; the King whispering
and the heralds paying little mind
to the back and arms, sweeping, tidying,
that are slowly becoming the King.

He died near dawn—everyone was asleep:

Àwòrán means a thing represented.
Rán is a compression of *ránti*: to recall—
as in recalling the subject, reminiscent of what is represented.

Awòran means watcher.
Ran is a compression of *iran*: spectacle.

The watcher remembers a spectacle,
the art that imitates asks to be an agent that recalls.
Compressed into the mirror of beholder and beheld
recalling and spectacle become the same syllable, with
     different passions of breath.
He died near dawn—everyone was asleep.

His shy corpse asked to be recalled.

The eye is an egg, with two parts that see.
The shell sees shapes and colors. *Oju lasan*, naked eye.
The yolk sees the same thing at the same time:

Aworokolokin's naked eye rolled in his naked body
as I buried him. He became a yolk, the inside eye, *oju inu*.
This eye becomes infatuated, casts spells: unintentional and
    intentional,
receives dreams: grafted on top of what is real, or when you
are asleep.

Aworokolokin
Ko ko—soft bird, ko lo, sweet bird.
His crown was like a fan of reeds,
it fell like a fan over his face.
It moved air like breath.

Imagine knights with visors:
they miss the point
and shout their names and the names of their loves
and make a cry like wet beans in a tin can,
small knights crammed into the same visor,
shouting of love, sliding onto a plate.
The King whispers
and the heralds pay him little mind.

I donned the crown.
Legend has it that a terracotta head passed for a king for a month.
I called in an artist to make a head of me.
Did you know that our stomach muscles are connected
as a remnant of when we were worms?
I move my stomach muscles as little as possible.

My crown is branches;
when an eye is upon me,
it settles on the branches.

I shall be the only one,
with time enough to remember
that I and the red, beating gods
punish differently, knowingly.

TROY

Tooth and tooth
Tooth and tooth
Baboon

There are tents where the sand
is made of lice
under the light of the moon.

Tooth and moon and tooth
Tooth and tooth
Baboon

They come,
they mate; it's ugly.

A circle of apes.
An eight of many brown apes,
around the white naked points of the tents.

In the corner of the tent are fine pieces of art, fine things.
A candelabrum melts, or the sand crawls up it.

The racket!
Inside the tents, the howls thud like food.
We need more room in our mouths.
The chef makes Eucharist of the food,
threading his hairs into the meats.
It's his only way.

The watchman, in his tall tower,
worries:
Every day he must make his yo-yo string
a little tighter.

BUSTAN

A land and its peoples are often spoken of together.
This is a description of just a land,
and not its peoples:

A bare tree here is not like
a bare tree elsewhere—
It does not have potential, nor is it dead.
It is a wrecked loom;
do not hang your wash on it.

I am offered tea at every place the paths meet.
The globe of tea is like a locked sun,
or a fish with a tail,
so good at being a tail
it reaches its head again,
and makes the head a tail,
until it is one round tail.

Tea, tea,
wise as the sea,
tell me how to be with child.
The tea instead offers
a steady stream of limbs.

Buddha says, "Fire, fire, put out the fire!"
Everything burns here,
but not like Buddha says:
not from a fire-hoop where the flames go in
as a halo over our heads,

Rather flames come from things taking the shapes
of hammers and nails and lumber.

The new day is slid underneath
the old days:
the clouds can hear only themselves,
the wind can hear only itself,
the old sky grows idiotic and dark, and becomes heaven,
the sun wrenches itself open:

Uruk before Eden:
Bustan before Garden:
Our variety before variety:
shame before shame-knowledge:
When shame was an entity
disconnected from imagery,
wandering between you and me,
wandering even from the body
into the tea,
into the brass doves,
into this autobiographical moment.

I must take full responsibility. Quite right. I will move on.

MOM MYTH

All the spears,
falling in the sky:
the wood gets to be wood
but metal is forced into abstractions
about blood and coldness.
Metal is like a father.

Our stomachs are empty for the first time.
We bite the breast, and a pink world issues milk.
Teeth, enabling the consumption of meats
and proper diction, come later.

Brains, brains, hungry brains.
Teeth, biting for so long, in excess form a smile.

A myth involving Jason and my mother:
He plants dragon's teeth,
and supposedly threw a stone in the midst
of the army that sprung up to confuse them into fighting.
Meat, however, is ultimately secondary.

It was my blue-eyed mother, on bended knee,
a sapphire thrown in their midst by Jason—
she was the source of their confusion:
her gaze broke open a nearby gorge
freeing ants that descended upon the men:
the men did a silly dance,
at once showing off for her and made jerky and anxious by the
    ant bites.

Under the freshly popping knees,
the yellow ligaments, the fizzing drumskins.

At the end, their missing teeth were like moths
each around light of their own blood.
It is unclear which landed upon which—
the red light, the yellow moths.

"I love you" or "Let's do it" he or she said to his or her partner, who is the gender you prefer to have sex with.

They took their hand and placed it on the organ you like best. It was very slimy or not slimy depending on what is appropriate. "You like that?"

"Yes, I do." Or, alternately, "No, stop!" but secretly they desired them to continue.

They had sex and orgasms. The orgasms felt like the best orgasm you remember.

"I love you" or "That was great" was said.

Then things concluded.

SHEOL

You have starred in my food for six seasons,
the sharper the flavor, the sharper you are
—you seem at home in sauces and greases.
There is little of you in dry turkey, day after day.

Sheol is watching the same show, with one word dropped
every time it's played. Faces go slack,
and soon enough it is just rooms of people
and suddenly they are in a restaurant,
and suddenly they are back at home.

Sheol is the precedence-taking of the mind
that observes you doing. But you keep doing.
You are more aware of doing
than you are doing—with great effort
you can will your focus onto the doing.
For the most part, doing consists of a queasy undercurrent.
In Sheol you become aware
of how easily automatized are the
most ardently felt of our endeavors.

They say that blood shall not cross the faults of the rock,
I don't know if this means
animals, fellow Jews, one's own blood:
I do know that I shall probably not see you in Sheol.

But I will slightly stuff my shirt, and pull on my teeth until
     they become crooked,
but mostly just think about
what it means to do these things.

TOO MUCH BREATH

Open the girl up,
fill her with air:
here is the first boat.

First it is one, on the boat for one:
pink shoulders making a slap against the wind.

For oars we used our own hands, which bumped one another.

The sea dried, and the sun set.
We were left holding hands;
the boat sighed and began to go into the mud.

A hill grew, and a house,
and we went inside and lay down to sleep.

Your eyes close, my mammal.
The smile on my face
is the triumph of your idea and quiet.

One day, I might find myself alone and quiet.

ATLAS

Sweating plants grow,
creatures eat the salt,
they eat each other to get at the salt.

Study Questions:
What does time mean to Atlas?
What is symbolic? Would you like a simile?
"Where are you?"

There is reminder in movement:
Bless stillness: it kills the phylum.

Atlas's suitcase is enormous:
it contains cures, as he recalls.
He can't look at it, looking as he must always look, at the sheep.

Don't. Instead
fall. Recite: *The sheep eats grass.*

BIG HAUL

In Spenser's "Epithalamion"
there are pagan cupids
setting traps in the bedchamber.

An excess of plaster made an eyeball on my ceiling.

The cupids took a mold of my hand, shaped for your ankle,
big to accommodate your big ankle.
They made lots of my wax grips,
and knocked on the windows with them,
used them to make more traps, and petted each other
with my hand.

Spenser declares he is "careless of their toyes"
but he spends ten lines talking about them,
and only gives one line to the "paradise of joyes":
prissily, the vagina.

The cupids dally amorously overhead,
and by watching them
I get to forget how big the situation is,
watch as they take you, the colossal swimmer:

they haul you in, aboard their
big gray vessel,
and gamble,
their wings rustling perfectly in time to the clatter of the dice.

C

Let's dream at each other:
like two crows learning the same face,
a face that scatters bread.
And we can eat the leavings of the dream,
and speak of that in the voices of crows.
The face's movement to smile or to weep
is us in the dream, having overcome blank sight to see one another
in this other place. Or if not to see,
to do what might be done in a dream.

I have spoken to you of heaven:
I simply meant
the eyes are suns that see;
seeing is the faces' nervous, delicious Lord.

Listening to you makes me naked:
when I kiss your ankle, I am silencing an oracle.
The oracle speaks from the hill of your ankle.

If we have the same dream, then perhaps I will open in front
        of you
and you can see the bright banner of your heart,
the firm joists of your heart,
the water of your heart,
dispersed through the channels and funnels
of what my body is.

US AND THE GOOD GUEST

You took a picture of the chocolates
brought to us by the good guest
so you could send him the picture of the chocolates.
Half-eaten by us happily at your perplexing insistence.

You did this to tell him he was a good guest,
and had been a good boy, who did a good job.
And look at how happy he had made us.
And how happy we can be.

THE OEDIPALEAN SABBATH

On all other mornings
I sat in my room until 9:00
and watched television at low volume.

But on Mondays I was allowed
to go into my mother's bed
and watch puppets on the television
at 7:00.

We were naming the standard poodle,
whose father was also his grandfather.

My father said,
"We need a special name for the dog, what is something special?"

"Mondays are special," I said.

We named the dog Monday.
He could fetch
and he died of cancer 13 years later.

POSTCARDS FROM MOUNT BLANC

Slept in loft,
Frenchmen fucking each other in sleeping bag next to me,
Oh, Antoine! Antoine! Michel! Mon dieu!
Opened window, it was stifling.
French believe cold air causes malaria.
Maldelaire! Maldelaire!
Tried reasoning. No fucking mosquitoes at this altitude.
He threw a piton,
and narrowly missed my neck.

French went to sleep. Had to piss
—no bathroom. Pissed out window.
Phil pushed me out.
Kept pissing as I fell.

Wish you were here:
rocks look like construction equipment
abandoned when the rules changed.

LET'S TALK ABOUT BANALITIES

Let's talk about banalities.

Today I psychodynamically arrived at conclusions fruitful to
my coping and moving forward from this period of mourning.
They are the same conclusions.

There is a bed,
sometimes the bed is very hot—
There is a dripping still life on the bed,
and you sip the water
and you eat grapes
and there are seeds in the grapes.
You discuss Zionism,
you discuss the artist's role in whatever—
It's so hot,
you lie in the bed,
it hurts your tummy.

Sometimes the bed is not hot,
sometimes it's a bed.

It is comforting to see objects
in the store that one has purchased in other stores
at great distances away.
Thus one confirms:
the strong lineage and pedigree of trucks and airplanes,
the closest we can ever get to destiny,
is consumer surveying.

There is no solitude; peace is risky: I am always accompanied
by this lamp that I am expressly forbidden to judge.

When you watch Barney, and he's waiting to speak,
his face is always perfect for what he's going to say,
and for listening.
To live like this! A blessing.

BUILDING THE TANK

I love them because I am good at them.

I thought of no rooms. In every stage of building, as I laid
down lines of glue, as I clamped the light, as I poured gray
pebbles, I saw life for them like detectives unburdened from
the duties of going from room to room.

To be good at them means that, one day, my shadow, that
difficult marvel, will pass through water, where there is no
light, and come to be a delectation, rippling into the fish that
are like wounds, feeding them closed, and bringing quiet.

TO C

We tended to a crow,
and now it's fine.
It shakes its head, and eats crickets,
forgetful bird
which you put in a pouch to make it sleep.

They said his eyes were blue because he was young,
and that black overtakes the eyes of crows as they grow old.
They lose focus and become more sensitive to motion,
disruptions in a lake of light.

If he were to see you now,
how could he recognize you?
I am a crow, and
I think you are mostly a pattern of motion,
and I am a leaf—and your hands fan under
and over me, and create a little space
in which the virtuous thing in my life
is my motion.

I think you can be traced
most easily by the echoes of your kinetics, my love.
Your lips, neck, arms,
these are not the harbor;
the you-around-you is the harbor.

In our bed, in the dark,
it is not sound, it is not outline,
but the motion of you
that brings to the surface of my body

all the apparentness of how I feel.
How I feel is then forgotten,
and instead I find myself
moving, joy, moving!

JANUARY 8

As you leave me you say,
"my mammal."

I'm hurt:
you offer the present.
So we continue to slash:
shrinking, ill, paired, drops.

The mixture the wrong mixture

of brain.

The smells flocking to the wrong parts
of the mind.

How long had we waited?
We traced, with sharp black glass points,
widening circles on the edges of the thin cliffs.

The crossing, dark loops were foot-widths apart,
as if to invite careless treks.

"Keep your heart open," you hear rightly,
your face curling up and out with rage.

Overhead, the green angels mutter,
oppressed by the thin cliffs of our souls,
mostly oppressing themselves.

I fix everything by dying, and you not dying.

LISTENING, SPEAKING, AND BREATHING

I.

Pianos are told to repeat
the grieving tones of a bird.

How does the bird focus?
How does the piano focus, in turn?

II.

Wind is a force through air.
Air is the soft gilding powder of the chest.

The soft gilding powder that departs
into the shaking mural of the blood.

III.

Sensing is not the same as essence.
Essence comes together with my voice.

Life might be very small victories and meanings.
Is saying "joy" a joyous thing, in and of itself?

IV.

Even if the tune seats the sense for an instant,
like a cloud through which blue is visible.

The red stripe of piping beef circling down
obnoxiously murmurs at death till it hushes.

V.

I have never listened alone.
Always a guide, a fabric of love and need, absorbing in the ear.

Even the unlistening God
listens more than your own life.

VI.

Love comes from the mouth or in the heart
open on both ends, a tunnel.

The impure love I make is all I know,
but its contents insist that there are others to make it.

VII.

The slender rod of my sense
pocks the angel as a grain in the snow.

The rod is praised to be alone:
memory binds shut the madness of the forking rod.

VIII.

The angel is told to repeat
the praise of the maker for himself.

The piano's voice is the white, grasping whole of the lily,
the angel's voice is the orange, stabbing whole of the lily.

IV.

If after the poem I am still an object,
then we'll know that, won't we?

I hope then you'll talk to me
and promise I make sense of you.

SKY-SEX DREAMS OF RANDAL

I am raving at you
with extremely good eye contact.

I fancy, lovely, that there are many drains
to circle.

Look at me and bore me,
bore me good and flaccid.

That's right, now I'm in a getup,
dressed like a palm-tree lady.

I have reached the end of suffering
and sat on the dark porch:

On the white ledge, a spider throws up the fat
of a bee.
Three white wood chairs in the mud,
a glass-topped table sealed into
a knot of pampas grass.
The chairs watching shadows on the glass top
like white poodles, all named "Handsome,"
from different phases in your life,
watching your sex-dreams play out.

Sob, elf.
Yelp, gnome, of the end.

HAPPIEST MOMENTS (AUTOCALIBAN)

I.

Very few memories, ultimately—happy and circumstantial.
Too rarely related to my brilliance.

Physical contact:
given and received absolutely and at all times.

Things were quiet,
and in me a long, awful note sounded
from the throat of the stork.

II.

I heard several months later the note:
it had gotten stuck in a tight channel between a gate
in my yard—small white lintels.

The note repeating over itself
had made it go almost a tan white.

I stuck my head in between the posts
and was surprised at how sympathetic my phrasing was.
It was still apt, and spiraled neatly, as if braiding my hair.

Eventually it pulled my hair out:
and I found to my surprise that one of my hands
was conducting with a dandelion pulled from under the fence.

LAST LIST

the speaking, dying thing:

"paddle. I've done that"

"press. I've done that"

a vague and distractible recurrence:

this mind and its sight:

mountainless snow

not filling-a-void,

held up.

echoes against

the small snowbirds

the white bodies, strapped with blood

stomachs rippling against the

words,

cold and roomless birds.

the skinny words that won't-be-honed,

lacking a frame,

an arc of black stone.

featureless:

how loved you have been,

how loved, and how unsound.

the changed body

You say:

"Plants: a pissing sun.
Mutts: tapetum lucidum, tapetum lucidum, tapetum lucidum.
Bats: a chiming feast of crickets."

To move is a disclosure

of what is around

and of what is essential.

Take no offense then,

at this tired old kitten

threading herself in the cracked white flowerpot:

clicking, surprising, shadows

on the white chalk sands.

TAGES

I hold my face
in the bed.

Me: *What is my future?*
Shon: *Flowers. You are marrying flowers.*

ACKNOWLEDGMENTS

I. The Final Voicemails

These poems have been previously published in the journals
below:
Berfrois: "My New Friend"
Boston Review: "Quiet Romance" (as "The Very Sexy Oracle
of Delphi"), "Anatomic and Hydraulic Chastity," "Nobody
Asked Anything," "Tuesday," "Delphi"
FIELD: "Uncle Needle," "December 29"
Horsethief: "My Bathtub Pal," "Your Next Date Alone"
Iowa Review: "Dinner in Los Angeles, Raining in July," "Lei-
sure-Loving Man Suffers Untimely Death"
Parnassus: "The Final Voicemails," "Earthquake Country
before Final Chemotherapy," "Down with the Landlord"
Plume: "Centaur Music"
Poetry: "The Soundscape of Life Is Charred by Tiny Bon-
fires," "Boy Goes to War"
Poets.org Poem-a-Day: "Cachexia"
A Public Space: "Amuse-Bouche"
Yale Review: "Name My Time of Death and See What I Do to
You"

II. Mammals

These poems appeared, in their final form, in *Four Reincarna-
tions*: "Troy," "Bustan" (as "The Hanging Gardens"), "C" (as
"Hi, Melissa"), "To C" (as "For Crow"), "Sky-Sex Dreams of
Randal," "Tages" (as "Second Dream").

Ashley Woo

MAX RITVO (1990–2016) was the author, with Sarah Ruhl, of *Letters from Max*. His first collection of poems, *Four Reincarnations*, was published by Milkweed Editions in 2016. His chapbook, *Aeons*, was chosen by Jean Valentine to receive the Poetry Society of America Chapbook Fellowship in 2014. Ritvo's poetry has also appeared in the *New Yorker* and *Poetry*, among many other publications.